The Couples Would You Rather Edition

Beckie Reid

© Copyright 2019 - All rights reserved.

The content contained within this book may not be reproduced, duplicated or transmitted without direct written permission from the author or the publisher. Under no circumstances will any blame or legal responsibility be held against the publisher, or author, for any damages, reparation, or monetary loss due to the information contained within this book. Either directly or indirectly. You are responsible for your own choices, actions, and results.

Legal Notice:
This book is copyright protected. This book is only for personal use. You cannot amend, distribute, sell, use, quote or paraphrase any part, or the content within this book,
without the consent of the author or publisher.

Disclaimer Notice:
Please note the information contained within this document is for educational and entertainment purposes only. All effort has been executed to present accurate, up to date, and reliable, complete information. No warranties of any kind are declared or implied. Readers acknowledge that the author is not engaging in the rendering of legal, financial, medical or professional advice.

The content within this book has been derived
from various sources. Please consult a licensed professional before attempting any techniques outlined in this book.

By reading this document, the reader agrees that under no circumstances is the author responsible for any losses, direct or indirect, which are incurred as a result of the use of the information contained within this document, including, but not limited to, — errors, omissions, or inaccuracies.

This book is not for minors. If you are not 18+ put this book back!

How To Play...

1) Have two or more people around (the more the better).

2) The person holding the book asks the question and the person listening HAS to answer one of the two options (no skipping).

3) Take turns asking questions (don't keep the book to yourself).

4) That's it, have fun!

In case you didn't know...

Angels Three-way: A guy with two women in bed.

Devil's Three-way: Two guys with one women in bed.

Ex: A former girlfriend, boyfriend, husband, or wife.

Golden Shower: Peeing on someone for sexual desire.

Hall Pass: When your partner gives you permission to see other people.

Hickie: A bruise on someone's skin from being bitten, kissed, or sucked too hard.

Nymph (Nymphomaniac): A woman with uncontrollable or excessive sexual desire.

PDA (Public Display of Affection): Can be holding hands, hugging, kissing, or groping without sex of any kind in public.

1

Would You Rather...

Your partner work late so you can't cuddle them at night

or

Work early so you can't wake up next to them in the morning?

2

Would You Rather...

Ask ten randoms on the street if you can give them oral

or

Ask one person who you work with if they'd give you oral?

3

Would You Rather...

Have sex with an erotica audio book on in the background

or

Have sex with porn on in the background?

4

Would You Rather...

Be with someone who uses too much tongue when they make out

or

Someone who doesn't use any tongue?

5

Would You Rather...

Get your partner off under the table at a family dinner

or

Rub them off in a crowded and busy restaurant?

6

Would You Rather...

Sleep with your boss at work for three months to get a raise

or

Sleep with three different people at work to get a promotion?

7

Would You Rather...

Cry when you orgasm

or

Accidentally poop a little every time you finish?

8

Would You Rather...

Rather have a naked picture of yourself surface the internet

or

Have a video of you having sex play on live television for a few seconds?

9

Would You Rather...

Have group sex with all of your exes

or

With a bunch of randoms you've never met before?

10

Would You Rather...

Be caught naked at school/work once in front of everyone

or

Walked in by your partner's parents masturbating once?

11

Would You Rather...

Be in bed with someone who asks too many questions

or

With someone who apologizes a lot?

12

Would You Rather...

Get oral sex in a public place if there was no chance of getting caught

or

Give oral sex in a public place?

13

Would You Rather...

Someone who shows a lot of PDA

or

Shows no PDA at all?

14

Would You Rather...

Accidentally upload nudes to your family's whatsapp group

or

Accidentally post a nude on Instagram and not realise for a few minutes?

15

Would You Rather...

Sniff your best friend's underwear

or

Wear your best friend's used underwear for a day?

16

Would You Rather...

Everyone thinks that your partner worked in the porn industry

or

That everyone thinks your mum was a stripper?

17

Would You Rather...

Accidentally send a nude to your boss

or

Accidentally send it to your mum?

18

Would You Rather...

Have sex when you're on MDMA

or

When you're drunk?

19

Would You Rather...

Have your ass eaten out

or

Eat out your partner's ass?

20

Would You Rather...

Your partner be more rough in bed

or

Be more gentle?

21

Would You Rather...

That your partner work at a strip joint

or

That your partner is the Madam at a brothel?

22

Would You Rather...

Not be able to shower for an entire month after a day of rough sex

or

Have no sex for the whole year?

23

Would You Rather...

Play with ice on your partner's body

or

Hot wax from a candle?

24

Would You Rather...

Do it in the changing rooms of a department store

or

Do it in the toilets of an aeroplane?

25

Would You Rather...

Discover your partner slept with their ex

or

Slept with one of your friends?

26

Would You Rather...

Have a porn star who's great at sex as a partner

or

Have a stripper who doesn't sleep with anyone as your partner?

27

Would You Rather...

Someone in bed who doesn't like giving head

or

Someone who only wants to have anal sex all the time?

28

Would You Rather...

Only be able to receive oral ever again

or

Only be able to give it?

29

Would You Rather...

Not be able to have another orgasm for a year

or

Have an orgasm every few minutes for a month?

30

Would You Rather...

Big boobs on a person

or

A big ass?

31

Would You Rather...

Give up making out with your partner for the rest of your life

or

Give up any foreplay before sex?

32

Would You Rather...

Use the pull out method, never catch anything but potentially get a woman pregnant

or

Always use protection, even with all your long-term partner's?

33

Would You Rather...

Have your parents sit on the couch getting semen on themselves but not know what it is

or

Have your parents see a bunch of used condoms and a dildo in your bathroom?

34

Would You Rather...

See your partner sleep with your best friend

or

See them sleep with your worst enemy?

35

Would You Rather...

Another girl in bed with you

or

Another guy?

36

Would You Rather...

Come home after a few drinks and only have sex once and no sex in the morning

or

Come home hammered, no sex at night but get to lie in bed and have sex all morning/day?

37

Would You Rather...

Be really bad at foreplay

or

Be really bad at sex?

38

Would You Rather...

Walk in on your partner's parents

or

Your partner's parents walk in on you?

39

Would You Rather...

Someone with massive muscles like a bodybuilder who's super inflexible in bed

or

Someone with a scrawny marathon runner body who can last for hours?

40

Would You Rather...

Get paid to have sex from an unattractive person

or

Pay to sleep with your perfect ten?

41

Would You Rather...

Have gentle and romantic sex for the rest of your life

or

Have rough and wild sex forever?

42

Would You Rather...

Finger/be fingered in an eight bed mixed dorm room

or

On a park bench in a quiet park?

43

Would You Rather...

Have a partner who's better looking than you

or

Worse looking than you?

44

Would You Rather...

An attractive person who's bad in bed

or

An unattractive person who's really good in bed?

45

Would You Rather...

Do it in the back seat of the car like the old days

or

In the back row of the movie cinemas?

46

Would You Rather...

Be in a relationship with someone to later find out they are your cousin

or

Never find out that you're related?

47

Would You Rather...

Have a really flexible partner that can do all sorts of crazy moves in bed

or

Be the flexible one yourself so you can do the crazy moves?

48

Would You Rather...

Have a partner put a screwdriver up your bum with the metal end

or

Have them insert it with the plastic end?

49

Would You Rather...

Someone who can't make you cum at all

or

Someone who does but also cums very quickly themselves?

50

Would You Rather...

A scratcher and biter in bed

or

A screamer in bed?

51

Would You Rather...

Your partner cum on your face

or

Pee on your face?

52

Would You Rather...

Relax and get a hot, steamy, oil massage

or

Tie your partner up and be able to do what you want to them for twenty minutes?

53

Would You Rather...

Rather be a good dancer and know how to strip tease to turn on your partner

or

Have your partner be a good dancer/strip teaser so you can watch and enjoy?

54

Would You Rather...

Masturbate and have your partner watch you

or

Watch your partner masturbate?

55

Would You Rather...

Get to have a model in bed for a night

or

Someone you'll have the best sex ever with?

56

Would You Rather...

Do it when it's three degrees celsius

or

When it's thirty degrees celsius ?

57

Would You Rather...

Watch a stranger have sex with a sheep

or

Watch a stranger get a horse off?

58

Would You Rather...

Hear that you're a bad at giving head

or

Bad at sex?

59

Would You Rather...

Have sex with someone whose just exercised and is sweaty

or

Someone who has just taken a dump and still smells from it?

60

Would You Rather...

Have a really weird and disturbing face when you cum

or

Make a horrific sound when you finish?

61

Would You Rather...

Choose an outfit for your partner they have to wear

or

Dress up yourself and surprise your partner to see the look on their face?

62

Would You Rather...

Have someone in bed who's got an amazing body with toned muscles but bad at sex

or

Someone great at sex but has an average body with a big beer belly?

63

Would You Rather...

Be on top while having sex for the rest of your life

or

Be on the bottom for the rest of your life?

64

Would You Rather...

Lose your virginity to another virgin

or

Lose it to someone who was really good?

65

Would You Rather...

Hear no noise throughout all of the sex until the orgasm

or

Hear a lot of noise and nothing for the orgasm?

66

Would You Rather...

Be with a virgin

or

Or with a sex addict?

67

Would You Rather...

Have sex in a jacuzzi and swap with the hot couple next to you

or

Have sex in a hotel pool while a crowd of people watch from the windows in the building next door?

68

Would You Rather...

Listen to your grandpa talk about all the women he slept with when he was younger for an hour

or

Listen to your grandma read aloud erotica for five minutes?

69

Would You Rather...

Watch your partner make out with a random person for five minutes straight

or

Listen to them have sex with a random stranger in another room for a minute?

70

Would You Rather...

Be able to get horny on command

or

Be able to cum on command?

71

Would You Rather...

Watch porn in a room full of strangers

or

Get drunk at a party and do a striptease in front of all your friends?

THE END

www.ingramcontent.com/pod-product-compliance
Lightning Source LLC
Chambersburg PA
CBHW071754080526
44588CB00013B/2234